BLOCKCHAIN

Essential Blueprint for Understanding the Blockchain Revolution- Learn the Technology Behind Bitcoin!

Joshua Welsh

Table of Contents

Introduction

Conclusion

Introduction

Congratulations on downloading *Bitcoin* and thank you for doing so.

The following chapters will discuss how you can use bitcoin, help you understand why it is all the rage, and teach you how you can use it to help yourself make a little bit of extra money on the side.

There are plenty of books on this subject on the market, thanks again for choosing this one! Every effort was made to ensure it is full of as much useful information as possible, please enjoy!

Chapter one

BLOCK CHAIN FUNCTIONALITY

In using block chain it is pretty safe to assume that any data that is there is going to be correct and that all of the users on the system are going to be able to agree and trust the data in terms of the balance that is found in their accounts based on the transactions that they do.

Looking at the system, you have no real reason to believe that the transactions even need to be put on block chain. Any and all data that is stored on the block chain, however, is going to be stored inside of the blocks as long as the source putting it there is trusted and does not alter the information and no one else can alter it either.

If a comment or document is attached to a payment that is done through block chain, then the entire program will send that with the transaction that is completed.

Regardless, after a transaction, it is added to what is called a block. Blocks are verified at different rates depending upon the implementation. Bitcoin blocks, for example, are verified every hour. Multiple systems verify the transactions taking place and come to a "consensus" as to what actually happened. The final version of the verified block is the one which all verifying computers agree upon. After a consensus is met, there is then a block that cannot be changed. So, if something goes wrong – on a big or small scale – and a transaction (or set of transactions) are messed up, there are only extremely drastic and large-scale measures which may be taken to fix it.

This, however, is only step one when you're talking about block chain. After the creation of a block, the program is going to store the security that is needed to ensure proper execution of the program.

Block chain has become very developed and sophisticated in its short existence. One such example is *smart contracts*.

Smart contracts are a way of "smartening up" the block chain transaction model so that it's not just "this goes here and that goes there at this time or that time". Smart contracts add another layer where you can add programs which execute and help to bring about options to the model.

Let's look at this example, if you place a bet on two different horses, the easiest way to make sure that both ends of the bet are upheld is to make out a contract. But, to ensure that the contract works the way that it is supposed to, you are going to need to create what is known as a smart contract that forces both parties to uphold their end of the deal.

In making a smart contract you are going to need three things.

- The money to be given to the appropriate party
- The bet that is being placed
- The results

The person who is closest or is correct is going to be the one that wins the money.

At the point in time that the winner has collected their winnings, the contract cannot be reversed thus making it impossible to cheat the system like some systems can be.

Should a company decide that they are going to sell all of their shares to the public, those shares are going to be divided out each year and the respective holders depending on how much that person holds. Every year the amount is going to be updated. However, when we address the situation with a logical mode of thinking, it should stay the same each year.

A smart contract makes it to where accountants are no longer needed being that everything is inside of a system and it is taken care of there. Any distribution that has to be done is going to be done automatically. A benefit of this is that there is no possibility that payouts are going to end up being administered wrong and it will never be overlooked. Plus, block chain will create a ledger that can be seen by an administrator.

Smart contracts can also be used when dealing with complex situations. Situations like this are going to be where a contract is required to make sure that the goods or services being offered are given to who they were offered to before payment is issued.

Chapter two

BLOCK CHAIN REVOLUTION

The whole of the financial sector has changed thanks to block chain. Block chain has made it more efficient - not to mention more secure - for finances to be dealt with. The technology that you find behind cryptocurrency has been one of the topics most talked about when it comes to finances in the last several years. About a dozen different institutions are trying to launch block chain to make their business more efficient.

The block chain system is decentralized and serves, in most cases, as a public ledger of every transaction that is made and completed. Due to all of the protocols, the ledger is not only one hundred percent accurate, but it is also secured from anyone trying to change it.

At the point in time that it was developed, technology and finance were starting to intermingle in a more critical way than ever, and block chain became the way to go when dealing with any documents that had to do with digital assets and the transfer of those assets. That is where smart contracts really come in handy. Due to the fact that reordering and automatic processes were made simple using block chain, the technology enabled organizations to be able to operate at a cheaper rate than they had been previously.

It is estimated that when the year 2022 comes around, thanks to the use of block chain, a major bank is going to be able to be see their expenditures reduced by around twenty billion dollars.

Plenty of financial institutions are looking into block chain and all of the opportunities that it offers which include currency exchange, settlement remittance, micropayments, and much more.

Chapter three

BLOCK CHAIN INVESTMENTS

Block chain has transformed many different business models in a number of different sectors. When you look at block chain it is easy to see that it is much like a digital spreadsheet that members of an organization use while working on a decentralized network.

Several different investors looked at it and figured that they would have the ability to make a profit off the technology that is behind block chain. But, because of the way that it is written, there are unique factors to block chain that you have to be able to understand. If you are used to traditional trading, you are not going to be used to this. There are many different levels that are going to be used when attempting to figure out the very complex block chain technology. With block chain, there are at least five ways that you can use bitcoin and block chain technology in order to make an investment that is going to benefit you later on down the road.

One: stockpiling coins

A lot of investors have already begun to stockpile gold in order to wait for the price that is projected to rise sometime in the near future. By contrast, other investors have begun to stockpile bitcoins. While both of them are going to have their advantages, they are going to use different investing techniques and principals.

Both assets are rare, but bitcoin is generated faster and the rate will decrease while technology reaches a limit of about twenty-one million coins.

Ultimately it will come down to supply and demand. Should the supply be limited, then the demand will increase which is going to cause the value to increase.

Two: penny stocks

Penny stocks are a common starting point for introductory traders, and most cryptocurrencies are traded on the stock market. Bitcoin is a well-known digital currency, but it is not the only option that you can use. Ether coins are just like bitcoins only they are going to work on a different system because they are competing with bitcoin. Some currencies are going to meet the needs that other currencies are not going to be able to meet.

For example, a few cryptocurrencies are going to be developed in order to help make other digital assets register by providing a security increase by allowing escrow services and other ways for the privacy to be increased

Three: crowdfunding with Altcoin

Crowdfunding is a method that is a mainstream method that is used when trying to raise seed capital for a number of different investments. Coins are not going to have to be used when doing crowdfunding, but they can be when you are dealing with bitcoin. With this method, you will have coins that are given to you before mining and they are going to be sold as an offering which will be done before the system is launched to the public.

Bitshares are also a method that is used when using block chain. Applications, as well as services, are going to be utilized when dealing with pre-sale methods to make sure that the funds are raised. Investors are going to be given the option to purchase coins with the expectation that the price will increase in the event that the service becomes popular with others.

Four: angel funding and start-up ventures

Angel funding is not a new concept, and neither are the start-up ventures. Variations are taking hold with the idea that start-ups can be invested in that are based on the technology that is used for block chain. Block chain is going to become popular with a number of entrepreneurs and the interest in it has increased thanks to the technology that is behind the cryptocurrency concept. New start-ups are going to require a whole lot of funding which will inevitably come largely from angel investors. Angel funding is going to be the next step to the block chain frontier.

You have to understand that there are going to be risks with any start-up. Since profits are going to have the potential to be massive, you should weigh both the pros and cons of any startup that you are wanting to deal with.

Five: pure block chain technology

The block chain technologies are on the rise. Companies are using the technology behind block chain and becoming well known names.

Global arena holdings is a company that uses leverages of block chain technology to get voting verifications.

Chapter four

HOW TO USE BITCOIN YOURSELF

We've talked a whole lot about the fundamentals of block chain and how it's structured. You may just be itching to use bitcoin, now! I certainly wouldn't blame you. Here are the steps that you can take in order to get started with bitcoin transactions:

Step one: set up your wallet

Off the computer, you are going to keep your money in your wallet so that other people cannot get to it. But, what are you going to do with your digital money that you cannot get ahold of physically? You' re going to put it in a digital wallet.

A mobile wallet is going to be run off of any mobile device. Wallets like this are going to be portable and going to be able to be used in stores. Since mobile phones are less likely to be hacked, they are going to be an environment that is more secure than a normal wallet.

Software wallets will be wallets that do not require a third-party service to be downloaded. The wallet is going to operate on your computer and all of your transactions are going to be run anonymously. Bitcoin was originally made to be used with this sort of wallet.

Web wallets are one of the most user-friendly wallets that are out there and they are going to be able to be accessed anywhere that you have internet access. All you will need to do is create an account and then log in. The only set back is that these are going to be less secure than the other wallets.

Step two: acquire bitcoins

Getting bitcoins is actually not as simple as it sounds, but there are a couple of different ways that you can get some. The system that you are going to be working with is highly unpredictable and still being experimented with, but that does not mean that there are not opportunities that you can use to gather bitcoins.

You can trade bitcoins with other people who are using bitcoins. The hardest part of this is to find someone who is interested in a trade. Most of these people can be found on trading sites and you will be able to sell goods or services to get these bitcoins.

Bitcoins can also be bought by visiting bitcoin marketplaces online. These transactions are going to mean that you need to spend money so that it can be converted to bitcoins, or that you're buying from somebody online who has bitcoins in the first place.

Lastly, you can mine coins. There are programs that you can download that will verify the block so that you can make a profit by just letting the program run on your computer. This was the technique that was used when block chain first came out, but it is not anywhere near as easy as it used to be. It takes a good computer and a lot of power to mine bitcoin now, and it almost certainly will be extremely taxing on your power bill. The only way it's profitable is if you have enough specialized computers in order to actually turn a profit. Some people have set these sort of things up: they're called bitcoin mining farms, and they're terribly expensive. Some smaller cryptocurrencies still have relatively simple and easy mining, but the problem with smaller cryptocurrencies is that they're, well, smaller.

Step three: make your wallet secure

Coins like money make it to where people are going to try and steal them. Your wallet needs to be secured so that people cannot get to your coins. The older clients of bitcoin that did not have the option to encrypt their wallets made it to where everyone could steal coins from the other person.

With the updates to technology, you can secure your wallet and protect yourself and your coins with encryption. You also have the option to use different wallets so that all your coins are not in one place.

Step four: spending

Bitcoins are just like normal currency when it comes to

spending them: you have to have somebody that accepts them to trade it. However, more and more places are starting to accept bitcoin as a method of payment. Normally, you pay by taking the *address* of somebody's wallet and sending money to them from yours.

Chapter five

THE FINANCIAL SERVICES INDUSTRY DISRUPTED

Block chain represents several hurdles to the traditional financial industry. The first of which is that block chain supports cryptocurrency and any services that are needed to support the use of cryptocurrency. That is to say that cryptocurrencies are generally always running on block chain, which presents another several competing modes of currency to the world.

Block chain also enables financial assets to be tracked inside of an environment that is completely secure and you do not have to worry about it being hacked or changed. Not to mention, the complexity of the transaction process is going to be reduced. This means that the "big brother" nature of traditional financial services and the typical record-keeping/third-party role of such institutions is no longer necessary.

Block chain makes it better and easier to manage the digital risks that are always going to be there with the financial industry. Ledgers are going to be created and sent out to those who need to see the ledgers and they are not going to be sent to anyone else. The processes that are being used when dealing with the risks are going to be sent to these people as well. On top of it all, it improves the processes that are in place for the networks that are needed in order to verify the history of any transaction that has been done.

Bitcoin was on the rise in 2012. that year, about a billion dollars were sent through the system. Its rate of growth since its inception in 2009 has almost perfectly mimicked an exponential graph as drawn on a graphing calculator. It more has been sent through the system and it is used more. There are a few companies that are trying to break into the bit coin market, while others are trying to improve on the services that they currently offer to their customers so that they can try and keep their customers and make their banking experience better. Sadly, all banks, no matter who they are, are afraid to break into the full use of block chain due to the fact that they are afraid of what it is going to do to their services and how it is going to affect their customers.

However, technology is constantly evolving and it is reducing the fees that are in place for a lot of financial transactions that are done on a daily basis. Not only that, but the risks that are involved with these transactions is being reduced when it comes to the exchanging of currency. Any payment faults or cut off times are going to be eliminated because there is no longer going to be the need to have duplicate documentation. So, there is yet another added benefit that you are going to be reducing the amount of paperwork that being printed out!

Those financial institutions that do invest with block chain are having to set up teams that are inside of their branches so that they can deal with any start up companies that are going to want to use block chain.

There are a lot of common mistakes that bitcoin is going to get rid of within the financial industry. Thanks to the fact that block chain can handle payments, there is a living document that the user can view in order to see when their payment is due and what is being paid out of the payment that they make. Like mentioned earlier, the need to have documentation is going to be eliminated as well because the documents are going to be saved on a node that is going to be accessed by the bank and by the customer.

Chapter six

BITCOIN

Blocks are essentially public ledgers, and in the case of bitcoin, these blocks are going to be created by the transactions that go through the block chain system. The system was made to get around the need for a "trusted third party" and thus does not require a central authority that everyone using the system trusts to make decisions. Maintenance is also going to be done by the network through the software that is being run to verify the block chain. Essentially, a live person is not going to be needed to do most of what block chain does which is going to eliminate a huge risk of human error; everything that happens on blockchain is the result of a bunch of computers essentially comparing homework answers to come up with a completely correct assignment, except the homework answers are the transactions and the completely correct assignment is the verified block.

The networks that validate the transactions before they are added to a ledger are going to be made after ensuring that the nodes are indeed available for broadcasting that the transaction has been completed properly. The proper verification has to be given to the bitcoin and that has to come out of the decentralized database where the block data has been distributed. Therefore, every node that mines bitcoin and uses bitcoin plays some part in the complicated process of block creation.

There are blocks created almost six times every hour whenever a transaction has been verified, added, or accepted into the chain. The software for bitcoin is going to aid in determining when amounts have been paid so that these amounts are not, for example, sent more than once when they aren't supposed to be. It is just another way for block chain to make sure that nothing is being overlooked.

Block chain ledgers are going to look at the data that is recorded for the transfers that are done on the system and sort them out by the notes that are located on them or the bills that are existing on a different part of the network. The coins are only going to exist in a form of currency that has gone unspent on the block.

Those who use mine bitcoins by verifying the blocks in the block chain have to "create" new blocks by verifying transactions. The maintenance is therefore done by the individuals who are mining rather than a centralized maintenance hub. Thus, for their efforts, miners are rewarded with bitcoin (or the currency of whatever they're mining.) Miners also have the ability to gain rewards for the transactions that they are able to verify and store into the blocks located on a chain.

Chapter seven

Smart Contracts That are On Block Chain

Smart contracts are probably going to be the aspect of block chain that will most likely be championed in the future. A smart contract is just a program that is activated once the block chain as a whole registers that a predetermined event has occurred. The smart contract is then given its own block and distributed as part of the chain.

While it may seem complicated, you can think of them in much the same way certain functions in a checking account work. In most checking accounts, automated deductions can be set up either by the user or by a third party with the user's permission. A smart contract works in broadly the same way, but from a decentralized—not centralized--position. Put another way; a smart contract is the computer code equivalent of the legalese in a contract that stipulates how and when all the little details are carried out.

Additionally, as long as the smart contract is generated on a public block chain, then, unlike in the banking example, there is no third party (such as the bank) who is able to step in and actively prevent the transaction from occurring. The transaction is equally secure if it is performed by a bank or by a block chain. This is due to the extreme type of security that is built into the block chain model, the fact that the data is decentralized, and the extreme cost required to hijack a block chain.

What's more, unlike with traditional contracts, smart contracts that are executed via block chain are completely public and viewable by anyone with a copy of the chain. This means that the smart contract is never open for debate or discussion; it is purely an expression of the facts as they are truly stated. This can be seen as a blessing or a curse, of course, depending on the nature of the information being made public.

A smart contract is where a computer protocol can facilitate, verify, and even enforce the negotiation and performance of a contract in which the contractual clause becomes unnecessary.

The smart contract can also have a user interface that will emulate the logic of a contractual clause(s). The proponents of a smart contract claim that many different kinds of the contractual clauses may thus be made partial or even fully self-executing, self-enforcing, or possibly even both.

Smart contracts are going to aim to provide the security that is superior to any traditional law contract. This will, therefore, reduce the transaction costs that are associated with the process of drawing up a contract.

Even with all that being said, it is important to know that a smart contract that is on Ethereum cannot retrieve data from the outside world. It can, however, ask outside actors to deliver the information on its behalf. Even at that, it either can trust what the outside actor says or verify the information given. This is just like when in court, the judge will ask the experts about their opinion or if a witness testimony can be verified by cross-checking.

So, it is, therefore, obvious that the computational resources for the Ethereum "judge" to be restricted by gas limit, which is low rather when being compared to the computational powers of the lawyers in the outside world. Even so, a judge can restrict in such a way that a way can still be decided when it comes to very complicated legal cases.

Ultimately, the contracts will be made on the Ethereum system based on the data within the system. If any outside sources need to be consulted, the system will have to choose between verifying the information or just taking the source at its word. This is more beneficial because it takes a player a's wishes for what they want to be done and holds player b to it via the contract.

This is just like any other contract that is made in the outside world, but it is online. The system will be in place until player a gets the work from player b that they requested. This also works with the payment method because the payment will not be sent until the contractual agreements have been met.

Common usage cases

With the rising market penetration of various financial technologies, smart contracts are becoming more and more prevalent. A big reason for that is because they are simplifying many common contract usage cases. For example, they are already making it easier for users to update various contract terms in real time, despite it taking days for physical copies to move back and forth to perform the same function. This not only increases the speed with which such processes can be performed but also greatly increases the odds of their accuracy remaining at acceptable levels throughout.

Smart contracts also activate automatically once certain real world conditions have been met, which means they require fewer resources to be utilized to the fullest. While this won't mean much to most users who use them infrequently, for business to business transactions, the savings will likely be substantial. The guaranteed and secure nature of a smart contract also means that it can be executed upon without the need for a third party to guarantee the transaction via escrow, reducing the closing costs of the contract on all sides.

Financial institutions will also find smart contracts useful in numerous ways. In regard to trade clearing or settlement scenarios, the final results relating to settlements, transfers, and trades is tallied automatically. Smart contracts can also be used when it comes to coupon payments, specifically to return principal on expired bonds. They also work with insurance claims as a means of minimizing errors and streamlining the flow of work between departments. Finally, they are also known to improve the regulation of Internet of Things services.

In the health care sector, smart contracts are known to offer up numerous advantages. For instance, they improve the accuracy with which medical records are updated as patients are transferred between departments. They can also be used to monitor the health of the population as a whole via public blockchains that update automatically and pay participants for using their information. Smart contracts are also already in use in many Internet of Things devices where they are used to determine the success of fitness goals and release rewards accordingly.

In the music industry, smart contracts are already being put to work tracking royalties for song usage and distributing payments accordingly. It is also being put to work on a smaller scale to enhance person to person interactions and is predicted to lead to things like trading energy credits and increased peer lending opportunities. This same technology is currently being adapted for use with the Tesla electric car, whereby users can charge at any charging station and be billed for the transaction automatically.

It is also changing the way large products are shipped and tracked by sending out automated documentation as various production pieces make their way through processing, and on to shipping. This can even be cued to the input of certain signatures, meaning the process is seamless for signing the contract to receiving the goods. Later on down the line, if there are questions about the quality of the shipment, then the entire route the product took from creation to delivery can be tracked. This is due to the fact that it is on the same block chain that enables the creation of the contract in the first place.

For credit enforcement, the smart contracts are becoming an extension of property law. The credit agreements are going to disable the product that you have purchased if you fail to make the payments that you agreed to make. For example, if you buy a new car on credit and fail to make your payment, hen the doors to your car are going to lock and then the car will drive itself back to the showroom.

However, most electrical products come with what is known as a kill switch that can be disabled should a condition not be met between the two parties. This would happen if the payments were being made through a public channel such as cryptocurrency.

The fact that a computer program cannot reliably tell you what is happening in the physical world or who is telling the truth in a situation is likely the biggest limitation with smart contracts. Checking to see if a bitcoin payment was made is a simple task that a computer can do. However, assessing the stipulations made in most contracts is much harder for a computer to do. A smart contract's execution is only going to be as good as the input that it is going to take in. But, it is going to be difficult to find out if the inputs are sufficient enough to do the job in such a way that both parties are going to trust.

The biggest solution to this is going to be to have oracles. Oracles are online service providers whose entire job is to broadcast the data that can be used as inputs to the smart contracts, as well as to the people who write them.

For example, if an oracle broadcasts the new entries on a government registry of the most recent deaths. The contract can pull out those who just had a living will or those who died because of natural causes.

When it comes to property law, the cryptocurrency can be thought of as a set of smart contracts. These smart contracts are going to be able to enforce property law. The cryptographic techniques are going to be used in order to ensure that only the owner of the cryptocurrency is the only one who can spend it. There are already several decentralized assets that exist. But, broaden out the range of assets so that there are different digital assets to be traded within a single block chain. When it comes to physical products such as electronic controls, then the same principle can be applied.

An early example of a smart contract is the Digital Rights Management technology, otherwise known as DRM. This contract does not take or even process the inputs. However, it does enforce itself by making it impossible for you to be able to break your contract by acting in an unauthorized manner. For example, copying something that is protected by copyright laws.

Finally, smart contracts also have the potential to make the voting process run more smoothly because smart contracts could verify a person's identity before recording their information. This information is safe from tampering and can be easily recalled if a situation arises that calls for a closer examination.

Financial sector

A smart contract works on what is known as a single ledger system, which makes it extremely easy for the program in question to determine if a specific piece of information is accurate or if it should be completely ignored. When implemented properly, they allow for the automatic approval of workflow and verification of calculations which, as a result, reduces lag and the potential for error. At the same time, it minimizes the cost and completion time of projects of all types.

Smart contracts also help with clearing trades, as I briefly mentioned earlier. As you may know, clearing trades manually is a process that is typically quite intensive. It involves a lot of labor time, and can even necessitate quite a few reconciliations both internally and externally. What's worse, each reconciliation brings with it, its own chance for discrepancies, which result in extra delays that cost even more time and additional resources. However, smart contracts smooth out this process considerably, as all the changes will be noted and updated automatically. The number of these types of transactions that are performed each year number in the billions, which means the market is primed and ready for smart contract intervention.

The single ledger format also makes it easier for the multiple steps in any supply chain to move along smoothly. The way it does this is by easily allowing a product to go through all the logistical stops prior to delivery without extensive physical verification along the way. This will be a huge boon to supply chains of all shapes and sizes, being that physical document related mishaps are routinely responsible for delaying packages 20 percent of the time. Smart contracts will also be able to deal with letters of credit and bills of landing automatically, simply as the package makes its way towards its destination.

In addition to making errors at times, old-fashioned transaction monitoring systems cost more than 10 billion dollars each year, so adopting a smart contract system will save suppliers and merchants a significant amount in the long run. As such, numerous major players in nearly every industry are currently looking into what they can do in order for a smart contract system to be a reality in their field.

Current limitations

Block chain is the database infrastructure of the future, and smart contracts are going to be at the forefront of its expansion. As such, it is important that those who are interested in using smart contracts to the fullest do what they can to prepare and promote new systems (their widespread use will be more than imminent). When looked at with a mindset towards the future, it is hard not to look at any process within a traditional business infrastructure that would not be improved by smart contracts that are deployed in the proper way.

Nevertheless, before you head out and begin investing exclusively in the smart contract market as it exists today, it is important to understand that there are still a few important issues that need to be resolved before the technology breaks through into the mainstream. First and foremost is the fact that many smart contract scenarios have been completed in usage scenarios that are small or medium-sized organizations; they are still largely untested in environments with a high volume of transactions such as in the traditional financial sector. If the public is ever going to fully accept the potential of smart contracts, they are going to need to see it working in action at the largest scale first.

Additionally, most smart contracts have no way of currently reaching information that is not stored within the block chain it is a part of. Some designers have discovered ways to include what are known as oracles, or access points to external information, into the smart contract, but the best way of doing so is still being discussed. This is not helped by the latency that a traditional distributed network faces, which can be as much as 20 seconds in some instances. While nowhere near the bottleneck it would have been a decade ago, this speed is still quite a bit longer than the milliseconds the same process could be completed in using a traditional server.

These issues combined have so far lead to few true examples of smart contracts being used in the real world. It's something else that needs to change if they are ever going to gain the wide acceptance they need to reach their true potential. What's more, the nature of how block chains store information means that once a contract has been written, it cannot be added to or amended in ways that were not in its base programming. The inability to make mistakes, especially while learning, will make it difficult for smart contracts to catch on without a mainstream reason for doing, so that appears viable in the long term.

Finally, one area where a traditional contract is still superior is privacy. While smart contracts created on private block chains don't have this issue, creating a smart contract on a public block chain means that everyone who is a part of that block chain will be able to see the details of the contract. This has potentially severe consequences for both individuals and businesses, as there is some information that the parties of a contract will naturally want to keep a secret.

Until this matter is settled, the general use of smart contracts across many contract types is likely to remain low.

Chapter eight

PROS AND CONS OF BLOCK CHAIN

When it comes to any given thing in this whole world, there are pros and cons. Block chain is not any different. Block chain is versatile and you can do several different things on it. However, when are you going to want to use block chain rather than staying with the traditional methods?

Being someone who uses block chain and bitcoin is going to protect your identity from theft, as well as your money. There is no need to put any of your personal information into the system so that a transaction can be completed, much like when you use cash. You also do not need to put in any card numbers, so that makes your card completely safe from anyone trying to steal it over the internet. Not to mention, you are not even going to need to put your real email address into any system; you are going to use, instead, the address that you use when you are doing bitcoin. Therefore, you can make an endless number of bitcoin exchanges without anybody knowing something personal like your e-mail address.

Payments can be sent and received with very little cost, if any at all. International payments are not going to force you to pay any transaction fees or exchange fees that you would have to pay when working with traditional financial services. This will also assist you when you find yourself traveling to other countries.

One of the biggest cons of block chain is that you cannot reverse a transaction once it has been made. If you send coins to someone by accident, you are going to have to receive a refund from the person that got the coins before they are spent. Other than that, the system is not going to do anything in an effort to help you not spend coins when you do not mean to. Along with that, block chain does not offer any liability protection for the usage of bitcoin. So if something happens for you to lose your bitcoins, then you are going to have to deal with it and add more security to your system to ensure that it does not happen again.

If you are going to keep your bitcoins, then there is the volatility that you are going to have to deal with. Over the course of time, you are going to notice that the value of bitcoins is going to fluctuate a lot so the longer you keep them, the less they may be worth whenever it comes to you actually spending them. For example, the typical price for a whole bitcoin is six hundred to twelve hundred dollars. If you keep your coins for an extended period of time, you are going to either make a profit or lose a large amount of money depending on how the market goes.

There are several companies such as Etsy and TigerDirect that accept bitcoins as a form of payment on top of traditional payment. Even some major companies such as Dell have gotten on board. However, most major companies such as Walmart and Target have not gotten on board yet, and there is no telling when they are going to get on board with bitcoin considering how well they are doing as it is. But, it is very likely that they are going to look into accepting bitcoins as the value of bitcoins goes up making it to where more and more people are using it.

Rather than being like a credit card, bitcoins are like cash. There are no extensions in warranty that you have to deal with, but then again, you are not going to have the rewards that you can get when it comes to using a credit card. Some places do not allow you to use a credit card for whatever policy reason that they have so then you are always going to worry about that as well. Then there are the fees and the added headache of the fact that if you do not pay it, it is going to affect your credit score.

Cash, on the other hand, is accepted everywhere. There are no fees. In fact, there are many times that you end up getting a discount because you used cash. With bitcoin, you are going to be able to use it without the headache of late fees or other things that you are going to have to worry about with a credit card.

The biggest similarity that bitcoins has with credit cards is the fact that it is not going to be accepted everywhere.

On the business side of it, using bitcoin is going to save you money. If you are going to use services such as Coinbase, then the first million dollars that you make by accepting bitcoins is going to be free for you. It is from here that you are going to begin to pay at least one percent on all of the transactions that you do. However, this is still going to be considerably less than what you are paying in order to accept credit cards.

Exchanges that are done with bitcoins can be converted easily without the need to worry about risking a lot of volatility. Not to mention, bitcoin eases any worries that you are going to have of chargebacks or even hackers getting into your system and stealing your customer's credit card numbers. The merchants that use bitcoin are normally going to work off of a tablet or even a smartphone when they are accepting a payment. This is an added benefit because you will not need a big fancy system that can only stay in one place. Therefore, you are going to be able to take your business with you anywhere and accept payments.

Although, if you are going to accept bitcoins, you should

make sure that you have a very clear policy on the returns of products that are bought by use of bitcoins. The amount of the return needs to be based on the dollar price that is on the item rather than the price that you sold the item at. This way you are not exposing yourself to the volatility of bitcoin.

All in all, make sure that you know the most recent developments that come with bitcoin so that you are not grasping at straws when they come out with new technology. The headlines that are out there for the software that is out should not cloud your judgment on cryptocurrency and the fact that you are or are not going to use it. Your best bet is to accept a variety of payments for your customers to choose how they want to pay for things. Plus you are going to be exposing yourself to less of an identity theft risk or the risk of credit card information being stolen. Plus, more customers are likely to come in your door because they are going to be able to choose how they want to pay and not worry about putting themselves in debt ot get the things that they need. To top it all off, you are going to be saving money on the fees you were paying before and protecting yourself from hackers.

Chapter nine

CRYPTOCURRENCY ON BLOCK CHAIN

Cryptocurrency or crypto asset is the medium that is exchanged using block chain technology in order to secure and pseudonymize transactions. Cryptocurrency is a currency which serves as an alternative to traditional currency. Bitcoin was the first major cryptocurrency, developed in 2009. Over the years, there have been several different cryptocurrencies that have been developed such as altcoins.

Cryptocurrency is decentralized which basically means that the currency itself isn't based out of any one centralized location or ran by any set of centralized figures. Which also results in the system not running at all like a normal banking system, which is actual a centralized.

The idea of anonymous electronic cash systems was first brought up in '98 by a Wei Dai which would end up calling it b money. It would not be too long before Bitgold was created which serves as a predecessor to bitcoin, one of the primary differences being that it requires its users to work with functions to find solutions. The solutions are then put together and published for others to see. This currency system was based on the purpose of reusable proof of work.

Nakamoto is the one who ultimately ended up creating Bitcoins synthesizing a lot of the previous proof-of-work developments with a new idea of the "block chain". However, in 2011, the namecoin system was created as a way to help with the DNS decentralization. It was not too long after the development of Bitcoin that Litecoin was released. Litecoin became the first cryptocurrency to use a hash function. The first hybrid cryptocurrency that was created was Peercoin and it used proof of work and proof of stake for its system.

Despite the fact that there are several different cryptocurrency programs that you can choose from, all of the ones that you have seen listed here are not still in effect today. It was in 2014 that the department of treasury in the UK decided that they were going to study cryptocurrencies and the role that they played on the economy.

It was also in 2014 that the second generation of the cryptocurrency programs were released to the public. Some of the programs were NXT and Ethereum. It was these programs that had the advanced functions that made it possible for things such as smart contracts and stealth addresses.

The very first bitcoin ATM was put up in Austin, Texas by Jordan Kelley in February of 2014. Much like normal ATMs, it had scanners, but it did not use them to scan an ID that was used in order to confirm their identity. Nonetheless, it allowed for users to have access to any cryptocurrency that was in their account at any given time.

Cryptocurrency has threatened the price of the financial institutes that have been around for what seems like forever. More trade is happening thanks to cryptocurrencies, which is going to end up causing consumers to lose faith in the currency that they have been using their entire lives. Due to the widespread use of cryptocurrency, it is also going to make it difficult for financial institutions to get the data that they need to see what activity is going on in the economy. One senior banking officer stated, "Widespread use of cryptocurrency makes it more difficult for statistical agencies to gather the economic data that they require."

Chapter ten

THE MYTHS OF BLOCK CHAIN

Being that block chain is still a mystery to so many, myths have sprouted up that surround bitcoin and block chain. But, many of these myths result in people who would otherwise invest inblock chain not investing because they suddenly become unsure about block chain. So, this is where some of those myths are going to be put to rest so that you are able to understand block chain just a little bit better and you may want to invest in block chain or bitcoin yourself if you have not already.

One: Block chain and bitcoin are failing

The person that you talk to will decide whether you hear that bitcoin is a failed currency or not; some think it has and some think it hasn't. The simple fact is that neither has failed by any measure of the word.

Plainly, block chain won't die for a long, long time. There is no reason for one to believe it will suddenly stop being used. It's a groundbreaking technology which enables decentralized structures where previously a third party was needed.

Bitcoin isn't failing, either. The reason people say that it's feeling is because there's some doubt about its ability to scale and the reality of it being useful on a large scale, similar to how people doubt the applicability of the language Esperanto on a global scale. That doesn't mean that it isn't, though. Bitcoin has a long and bright future ahead of it.

Two: thousands or tens of thousands of merchants use bitcoin

While this would be amazing, this is not true. In fact, there are very few merchants out there that accept bitcoins for payment. Somewhere around eighty percent of the currency on bitcoin is used for nothing more than speculative hoarding. If a merchant allows for you to pay with bitcoin, then what they're actually doing is partnering with someone who will turn those bitcoins into traditional currency. However, in doing this, any risks and fees are going to be placed on you rather than the merchant.

The few merchants that are looking into accepting bitcoins as payment are going to have to check how it works to see if it is going to work for them. But they are mostly doing it just so that they can get more exposure through the media and thus get more customers into their stores.

Three: bitcoin transactions are processed in real time like many banks process their transactions

Wrong! There is about a ten minute delay between when transactions are actually processed on the block chain. So ultimately, less than two transactions are done per second with bitcoin. However, this should be contrasted against many banks which process transactions through a clearinghouse. A proper bank transfer can take at least 24 hours. Bitcoin and other block chain cryptocurrencies don't have this intermediate factor, so the transactions can actually be a little bit faster.

Four: the transactions done on bitcoin are "nearly free"

Wrong again. There is a processing fee that comes along with using bitcoin but it is not charged to the users or the merchants.

Those who choose to mine bitcoin are going to be processing the transactions that are constantly occurring. The people who mine bitcoin and process transactions often make a small amount off of this, but they also are often paid a fair amount from bitcoin transactions.

As an aside, this process of mining is going to keep going up until around twenty-one million bitcoins are mined which is estimated to happen sometime around 2140. But, after that, there is no set plan that is going to tell people what the transaction costs are going to be.

Those transactions that are processed are rewarded minimally through the network via small amounts of bitcoins. It is this that represents the actual revenue that a miner receives. It's very rare that a miner's rewards are going to justify the high costs for investment and operation that it takes for mining. The intent is to have the cost of the transaction take the total cost for mining into account so that no one is getting left out.

Five: bitcoin is more secure than other currencies.

It is true that bitcoin holds a high resilience to any attacks that might come its way. But it is just like most other transaction systems that are going to have breaches in security due to human error or fraud.

In 2015 alone there were:

- Three hundred and eighty-seven million dollars that vanished from a bitcoin exchange in Hong Kong
- Thanks to a phishing attack, two millon dollars in bitcoin were lost.

- The bitcoin exchange in Canada was shut down because someone compromised their database.
- Trading was temporarily suspended because of one wallet in the operation was compromised thus compromising the entire system.

Six: the ecosystem for bitcoin is decentralized

The mining pools for bitcoin have increased some. At least one of the top four bitcoin mining pools is in China on their bitcoin exchange. The larger mining farms are going to artificially limit themselves so that democracy does not show any favoritism in the system. But, those that work with smaller mining pools are being driven out of business by the larger ones. It is like with any other system, the bigger you are, the more money you can spend and thus you are going to end up controlling the market.

One of the reasons behind this dominance is because it benefits the companies that are pushing out competitors: when more money is invest into bitcoin generation, it becomes harder to mine bitcoin and starts to take more processing power. The larger mining farms have all the money that is necessary to invest and operate and keep operating while other ones are being shut down because of how high the costs are.

There are a few opaque players that are controlling bitcoin and this allows them to be able to modify the transaction rules, thus making it harder for others to get into the investments because they are not able to keep up with the ever-changing protocols.

Think of it like the schoolyard bully that is losing at a game, but he keeps changing the rules because he does not want to show that he is losing. This makes it so that in the end, the rules always end up getting changed to where the bully wins and you lose. It does not seem fair, but you are not going to argue with the bully because they are bigger and can hurt you.

Seven: bitcoin is nothing more than idealistic and is not profitable

There are millions of dollars that have gone into investments with bitcoin. Somewhere around five billion dollars has already cumulated into the bitcoin currency to get it up and running for other sto use. Along with that, there are also other billions of dollars that are being invested for exchanges, bitcoin wallets, and the operation of miners.

Just a few examples are:

Fifty million dollars has been invested in a startup called Circle by Goldman Sachs

- One hundred and sixteen million dollars has been raised by VC in Silicon Valley for a stealth mode to be placed on bitcoin.
- The Coinbase program has raised somewhere around one hundred million dollars for bitcoin to use for operations.

Eight: Block chain is secure

There are features that are put into place for the writing of data because of the proof of work that is needed for block chain. Blocks have to be added to the chain and then the transactions have to be validated that are placed on that block before any repeat calculations can be made so that numbers can be located that make your block accepted by block chain and useable by other users. Plus it is going to be expensive if you are going to try and mine your own subversive chain.

The block chains that are private, in order to be secure, must have mechanisms that will replace the need for proof of work so that there is a limit to the ability that others have to subvert the chain that you create. In other words, block validators are going to need to be created.

However, rules are going to end up making sure that the blocks are specified for what has to be signed in the list of signatories. The list has to be limited which makes sure that entries take turns in writing blocks so that there is enough to go around. Bad behavior is going to be discouraged and limited thanks to this round robin style of work.

Nine: block chains are encrypted

Several different cryptographic methods are used with bitcoin as well as with the data that is encrypted and stored on block chain. Because of this, many people believe that all of the data that is stored on block chain is encrypted. However, this is not true.

Most of the data that is on block chain is actually unencrypted being that the data is going to need to be validated by the nodes. So, you are able to look at all the transaction data that is on the block chain servers.

But, the biggest problem with the encryption of data is going to be that it cannot be validated by the nodes because the nodes are not going to be able to unencrypt the data and see what they are supposed to be validating.

While using a private chain, the nodes are going to be able to be decrypted through the use of decryption keys. If you are doing this, you are going to need to think out why you are encrypting the data in the first place.

Research with cryptographic is constantly revealing solutions that are going to show that data that does not have any underlying data is known as zero knowledge proofs. When looking at this technology, you are going to come to realize that it is not fully matured yet.

Privacy is important to everyone, but what should you encrypt when it comes to block chain? Should the data that is in motion be encrypted? The data that is resting? Or should the whole database be encrypted? And then, when it is encrypted, who is going to have access to the data? When is it going to be decrypted? Can someone's permissions to the data be revoked?

Management of the data is crucial to the security of the data that is on the server. When the data is freely shared between two different parties, it is going to be even more crucial. So, carefully consider the security of the data that is in the block chain solution so that what needs to be protected is protected while still getting it validated by the nodes.

Ten: the middle man is erased and block chain users are allowed to do peer to peer on their own

This myth both is and isn't true. It really depends.

Technically, any two users can partake in "peer to peer", and the nature of block chain technology does indeed facilitate peer to peer trading by enabling people to technologically "join hands" without the need for a middleman there. However, peer to peer can have many meanings.

What it really comes down to is the question of how you define "middle man". The entire notion of "block chain" came up because there was a need to get rid of the idea of a "trusted third party" and simulate cash exchanges with digital currency. And in a way, block chain and bitcoin meet that ideal.

The problem before block chain and bitcoin was that every means of digital currency exchange – PayPal, online bank transfers, and so on – required that there was an intermediate service in order to determine how much money was moved and from where, as well as to facilitate the transaction.

Bitcoin and block chain invalidated this notion by making it so that the validations were *public* and *publicly validated*. This concept made it so that the trusted third party was no longer needed.

However, digital currency exchanges aren't at all like cash exchanges. In a cash exchange, the money itself serves as a bit of a middleman, because it can't be duplicated. On digital systems, this sort of thing isn't possible. So instead, the power of dictating who has what money and where money is going is delegated to the public at large rather than a single financial institution.

So if the question is whether bitcoin and block chain have a middleman, the answer is *no* in the sense that your money isn't going through a clearinghouse and there's not somebody keeping track on a ledger of everything.

However, the system by its very nature makes every bitcoin miner a middleman, in that they are necessary in order to process the transactions.

Eleven: block chains can be run off a user's phone

Using your phone to store block chain data is something that needs to be approached with caution. In using a phone, the phone will continuously chat with the rest of the block chain network while downloading and uploading other user's data non-stop in order to stay in consensus.

Chapter eleven

Gloassary of Block Chain Terms

Knowing what some of the words that you do not know is going to help you along in your investment with block chain. Here are a few words that you may hear but not understand.

Address: this is used to receive as well as send transactions on the network. The address is going to contain a string of alphanumeric characters as well as contain a scannable QR code. The bitcoin address is much like a set of keys. There is going to be a public key that a user is going to hold in order to sign their transactions digitally.

Bitcoin ATM: a bitcoin ATM is much like an ATM. It is a physical machine that is going to allow a customer to purchase bitcoin with their own cash. Many manufacturers are enabling users to sell bitcoins for cash as well. Sometimes these are called BTMs or even Bitcoin AVMS.

Bitcoin Price Index (BPI): BPI is a representation of the average price of bitcoin across the leading global exchange. But, it must meet the criteria that has been specified by the BPI.

BitPay: this is a payment processor that is used for bitcoins. It works with merchants by allowing them to take bitcoin as payment.

Block chain: there is a full list of blocks that have been mined since the bitcoin cryptocurrency was started. The blockchain was designed so that every block holds a drawing on the blocks that came before it. This was designed in order to make I tamperproof.

Block reward: this is a reward that is given to the miner for successfully completing a transaction block. There is going to be a mixture of coins as well as transaction fees that are going to follow the policy of the cryptocurrency that is being used. It will also be dependent on if all the coins have been successfully mined. For every block that is mined, there is a reward of twenty-five bitcoins. The block is going to give half of the reward until a certain number of blocks have been mined.

Client: the client is a software program that is going to run on a computer or mobile device. This is going to help connect the computer or mobile device to the bitcoin network and forward the transactions.

Cryptocurrency: a form of currency that is solely based on mathematics. Cryptocurrency is not printed currency, and it is produced by the solving of the mathematical problems that come from cryptography.

Cryptography: using mathematics, cryptography is able to create codes as well as ciphers that are going to help conceal any information so that it can be verified and secured.

Exchange: the central resource used for exchanging different forms of money and a variety of other assets. The bitcoin exchanges are going to be used to exchange cryptocurrency. Normally it is used to trade fiat currency.

Fiat currency: this currency is made out of thin air and only contains value because people say it does. Fiat currency is under close scrutiny by regulators because of the known application it has in money laundering as well as various terrorist attacks. This is not to be confused with bitcoin.

Hash: Hash is a mathematical process that is going to take the variable amount of data that it is given in order to produce a shorter output. The hashing function actually has two very important characteristics. First, it is mathematically difficult to be able to work out what the original input was by simply looking at the output. Next, in changing a small part of the input is going to give you an entirely different output.

Hash rate: the number of hashes that a bitcoin miner can produce in a specified amount of time.

Input: the bitcoin payment comes from this part of the bitcoin transaction. Usually, the bitcoin address is going to be the input unless a transaction generates one.

In simpler terms, unless the bitcoin is mined, the input is going to be the bitcoin address.

KYC: Know your client/customer.

Mining: this is the act that is known for generating new bitcoins. This process is done by solving the cryptographic problems through the use of computer hardware.

Node: when a computer is connected to the bitcoin network, then the client will be transmitting multiple transactions to the clients.

Output: the final destination where the address is going to be in a bitcoin transaction. A single transaction can have multiple outputs.

Pre-mining: a coin can be mined before the coin has even been announced. Pre-mining happens to be a common technique that scamcoins use. But, pre-mined coins are not always going to be scamcoins.

Private key: an alphanumeric string that is kept private by the user that it is assigned to. It is meant as a means of sending out a digital signature when hashed with a public key. In many cases, this string is going to be a private key that is designed in order to work with a public key. The public key is going to be the bitcoin address.

Proof of work: a system ties mining capability to computational power. The blocks are going to need to be hashed with an easy computational process. But, there is an additional variable that is going to be added to the process that is going to make it more difficult. Once a block has successfully been hashed, then the hashing is to be the proof of work that is needed for a block be validated.

Public key: this is a key that is publicly known with a hashed block. It is also known as the bitcoin address.

Scamcoin: an altcoin that is produced for the sole purpose of making money for the originator of the coin. These are often used in pump and dump techniques as well as pre-mining.

Transaction fee: there is a fee that is imposed on various transactions that happen on the bitcoin network. This fee is going to be award to the miner that successfully minds the block that holds the relevant transaction.

Wallet: this is a method used for storing coins for later use.

Conclusion

Thank for making it through to the end of *Bitcoin*, let's hope it was informative and able to provide you with all of the tools you need to achieve your goals whatever it may be.

The next step is to start using block chain and bitcoin for your investments and personal expenditures and begin to see what a difference it can make in your life. You are going to be part of an elite group of people that are going to be using block chain and cryptocurrencies since not many people use them yet!

It is going to be confusing at first as to how block chain works, but in the end you are going to be able to figure it out! Do not give up faith because you are going to be able to figure it out and keep going.

Also, do not allow for the myths that we discussed to get in your way of wanting to invest with block chain. While there are always going to be risks that you are going to face when it comes to anything, block chain is probably one of the safer bets being that it is less touched by human error.

Finally, if you found this book useful in anyway, a review on Amazon is always appreciated!

Thank you and good luck using block chain!

www.ingramcontent.com/pod-product-compliance
Lightning Source LLC
Chambersburg PA
CBHW071759170526
45167CB00003B/1094